Prudhoe Bay, Alaska

ARCTIC NATIONAL
WILDLIFE REFUGE

Arctic Village, Alaska

PORCUPINE RIVER

CANADA

UNITED
STATES

Oxnard, California

TIJUANA RIVER

Tijuana, Mexico

Hopi Indian
Reservation, Arizona

SAN IGNACIO LAGOON

SEA OF CORTEZ

MEXICO

Mexico City, Mexico

Milwaukee,
Wisconsin

Chicago,
Illinois

Woods Hole, Massachusetts

Westerly, Rhode Island

New York City, New York

APPALACHIAN MOUNTAINS

OHIO RIVER

Parkersburg, West Virginia

Whitesville, West Virginia

Old Diamond, Louisiana

Destrehan, Louisiana

MISSISSIPPI RIVER

LOUISIANA
WETLANDS

GULF OF MEXICO

To David, Michael, and Anna —H. R.

To my parents and Nicholas Brown —J. M.

Book design by Natalie Davis.
Typeset in Scala Sans.
The illustrations in this book were digitally rendered.

Text copyright © 2009 by Harriet Rohmer.
Illustrations copyright © 2009 by Chronicle Books LLC.
All rights reserved. Published by Scholastic Inc., 557 Broadway, New York, NY 10012, by arrangement with Chronicle Books LLC.
Printed in the U.S.A.

ISBN-13: 978-0-545-27446-3
ISBN-10: 0-545-27446-X

4 5 6 7 8 9 10   23   19 18 17 16 15 14 13 12 11

HEROES OF THE ENVIRONMENT

True Stories of People Who Are Helping to Protect Our Planet

By Harriet Rohmer
Illustrated by Julie McLaughlin

SCHOLASTIC INC.
New York   Toronto   London   Auckland
Sydney   New Delhi   Hong Kong

CoNTENtS

INtRODUCTiON

On a beach in Southern California, a teenage girl from
Mexico becomes a leader in the fight to protect her town
from a dangerous polluter.

In the far north of Alaska, a woman
sets out to save a herd of 110,000 caribou.

A young man from New York City finds ways to reuse
trash from construction sites so it stays out of landfills—
and brings money and jobs to his community.

Here are the true stories of twelve amazing people from across
North America who are dedicating their lives to helping the environment. Some of them work to preserve wild places like the Arctic
National Wildlife Refuge. Others work to make cities like Milwaukee
and Chicago better places to live. Some protect the habitats of animals, and others protect communities where people live.

In every story, you're right alongside the heroes as they take on
the problems, overcome obstacles, and find success. In the mountains of West Virginia, you'll travel with a coal miner's daughter

as her grandson inspires her to join the fight against mountaintop removal coal mining—and to start to build a "wind farm" to make energy from windmills.

You'll follow along, step by step, as a teenage boy and his classmates in a small Rhode Island town develop a recycling program for computers and other forms of electronic waste ("e-waste"), and advise state officials who pass one of the first e-waste disposal laws in the United States.

These twelve heroes represent just a few of the many people who are working today to protect the earth and all its residents. Their stories will inspire you, and you'll learn how you can support, join—and even lead—efforts to heal our environment, and keep it clean and healthy for generations to come.

ONE

Raising Food in the City

"Growing food is powerful.
It can change the world!"
WILL ALLEN
Founder, Growing Power Community Food Center
Milwaukee, Wisconsin

At 6 feet, 7 inches, Will Allen was a natural at basketball, and that's where he saw his future. An All-American player in high school, he received scholarship offers from more than a hundred colleges. He finally chose the University of Miami, and in 1967, he became the school's first African American athlete.

Going away to college meant leaving the family farm outside Washington, D.C., where he had grown up. He remembered how hard that life had been—selling vegetables door to door at age six, working long days as a teenager when his friends were out having fun. Now that his life was full of possibilities, he swore he would never go back to farming.

After college, Will turned pro. He married, had children, joined a European basketball team, and traveled to Brussels, Belgium, with his family. With time on his hands between practice sessions and games, he found himself visiting the Belgian countryside and hanging out with Belgian farmers. They farmed the way his parents had back home, caring for the land without using chemical pesticides and fertilizers.

"When I told my team manager I wanted to grow food again," Will remembers, "he got me a place in the country. Before I knew it, I had a big garden and twenty-five chickens."

Will Allen at Growing Power Community Food Center, in Milwaukee

A few seasons later, Will brought his family back to the United States. He took a sales job with a big household product company in Milwaukee, Wisconsin. After work and on weekends, he started growing food on land owned by his wife's family in Oak Creek, outside the city. Some of the food went straight to his dinner table, and the rest he sold.

Then one day in 1993, while he was driving home from work, Will spotted a FOR SALE sign on the last remaining farm in the city of Milwaukee. The place was small, only two acres, just a few greenhouses on a plot of land in a partly residential, partly industrial neighborhood. Ideas flashed through Will's head. He could grow food here. He could build a training center for kids. He could farm full-time. He saw an opportunity, and he grabbed it.

But he didn't start farming right away. "To farm inside the city, the first key piece is to be anchored into the city. You have to get to know people. They get to know you." Will started learning about his new community and becoming a part of it.

Most people in the neighborhood were not eating well. The supermarkets had moved away to richer neighborhoods where they could make more money. The little stores left behind sold mostly cigarettes and alcohol and food with lots of preservatives that wouldn't go bad on the shelves. The only way to get fresh fruits and vegetables was to take a long trip to the supermarket across town. "Folks were living in what I call a food desert," Will says. "I knew I had to do something, because you can't have a healthy community without healthy food."

He set up a farm stand to sell tasty greens and vegetables from his Oak Creek farm—at prices the neighbors could afford. He taught the kids some new basketball tricks, too. "A good player always knows where he's going," he told them. "He just doesn't always know how he's going to get there." Will was becoming part of the community. People trusted him and wanted to help him realize his dream of growing healthy food right there in the neighborhood.

With funding from a local church, Will hired some neighborhood teenagers to help him get started. Their first job was to "grow" new soil, because the soil in the old greenhouses was contaminated by pollution. Will showed them how you can create soil by composting, which means collecting different kinds of food waste and piling it up until it rots and turns into soil. Will explained that when you make compost out of local materials, different businesses in the city can help one another.

"In Milwaukee, we have a lot of breweries, so I used the waste from making beer. It's great stuff. We also got food waste from grocery stores, and I hooked up with a coffee seller and got the old coffee grounds." Letting Will take away all this waste helped the beer breweries, the grocery stores, and the coffee sellers avoid expensive trips to the dump. So everyone benefited. "We have wonderful soil now," Will says. "You throw a seed over your shoulder and it grows."

Will brought in thousands of pounds of worms to help fertilize his new plants. In a process called vermiculture, he spread layers of worms between layers of compost (lasagna style). The worms ate up the compost and pooped out what's called "worm castings." Amazingly, this worm poop doesn't smell bad at all, and it makes the best fertilizer in the world.

After making good natural soil (out of beer waste and coffee grounds) and the best possible fertilizer for plants (out of worm castings), Will and his teenage helpers, along with volunteers from the neighborhood, started growing food.

A student at Will's farm in downtown Chicago

Today, years later, Growing Power Community Food Center is a miraculously productive model farm, growing enough food to feed two thousand people on just two acres in the middle of a city. All the vegetables are grown in greenhouses. Pots of leafy greens—lettuce, sprouts, arugula—hang everywhere. Big bags of compost sit in the corners of the greenhouses. Milwaukee gets very cold in the winter, but the compost gives off heat as it breaks down into soil—enough heat to keep the greenhouses warm during the months when temperatures dip below zero and the ground is covered with 8 inches of snow.

Kids from the neighborhood come to the farm for tours and work-shops. They learn to prepare soil, plant food, and take care of the goats, chickens, and turkeys that live behind the greenhouses.

Herbs and greens grow in containers in the
Milwaukee Growing Power greenhouse

Some neighborhood kids are amazed that this is really a farm. "Farming in the city? Are you crazy?" Even more amazing to them are the thousands of red-eyed tilapia fish swimming in long aquariums at the center of the greenhouses. "Fish? What are fish doing in a green-house?"

The fish are for eating, but they also help the plants grow. The water they swim in, enriched by the fish droppings, is channeled toward the pots containing vegetables. Then it is drawn off, filtered by other plants, and returned to the fish tank as pure water. "We don't waste anything here," Will says. "It's like a forest. Nothing is wasted in a forest."

Over the years, Will's organization, Growing Power, has continued to expand. In 2002, he hired more people and opened an office in nearby Chicago, Illinois, to manage three city farms. At the Grant Park farm in the heart of downtown Chicago, Will and his staff teach young people how to grow more than 150 varieties of vegetables, herbs, and edible flowers. The Growing Power staff also runs garden projects in schools, where kids learn the basics of growing food and then get to farm their own plots.

People come from all over the world to learn Will's techniques of city farming—sometimes a thousand people a month visit the Milwaukee farm. Will also travels across the United States, Africa, and Central Asia to help people grow food more efficiently in ways that fit in with their own culture. "We're in a worldwide food crisis right now,"

Students harvest vegetables, herbs, and flowers

he says. "A lot of people are hungry. We need to grow food everywhere we can—in backyards and side yards, on rooftops, and even in buildings."

Will's vision for the city farm of the future is a multi-storied building, angled toward the sun. This idea, called "vertical farming," is a new way to help feed more people. "You grow fish on the bottom floor and pump the water up to the top floor. Then the water is piped down from floor to floor, through beds of growing plants. You're growing food on every floor, leafy greens up high, mushrooms in the basement. By the time the water returns to the fish on the bottom floor, it's clean again." In the back of the building would be production space, classrooms, offices, housing for visitors, and a store where people could buy the freshly grown food. He says that each building like this could feed thousands of people.

"Growing food is powerful," Will says. "It can change the world!"

TWO

Discovering a New Way to Clean Polluted Water

"Technology helped create our problems,
and technology can help solve them."
KELYDRA WELCKER
Student Chemist, Environmental Scientist, and Inventor
Parkersburg, West Virginia

Kelydra (pronounced key-LEE-dra) Welcker has always loved the Ohio River, which flows by her hometown, Parkersburg, West Virginia. As a matter of fact, she is named after the American snapping turtle that lives in the river, *Chelydra serpentina*.

"That's my real first name that my parents gave me," she says. (They changed the spelling from Chelydra to Kelydra.) "I'm a water turtle, and you have to take care of your namesake, right? I'm also an Aquarius, which is a water sign, and I've always cared about water quality. That's my work."

With a father who is a chemist and a mother who is a biologist, it seemed natural to Kelydra to learn how the world worked by doing

science experiments. She was in kindergarten when she performed her first one, an attempt to see if she could grow algae in the dark. She couldn't. "That's how I learned about photosynthesis," she says. "You need light to grow things."

At the age of six, Kelydra joined the Ohio River Cleanup campaign and came to realize how polluted the river was. In middle school, inspired by two famous women environmental scientists, Rachel Carson and Theo Coburn, she set up her own lab in a trailer behind her house. She began studying the effects of chemicals in the river water on the breeding habits of mosquitoes.

Kelydra was 15 when news broke about a chemical in her town's water supply that might cause cancer. The chemical, called C8, was a by-product of Teflon, the material used to coat frying pans so food won't stick to a pan's surface. People were angry and scared. Some of them blamed the chemical company upstream from their town on the Ohio River. The company admitted that yes, they had been releasing C8 into the river, and it was possible that tiny amounts had ended up in the water supply. However, they said, the quantities were so small that there was absolutely no danger.

Kelydra watched the debates about the problem on television and wondered what she could do to help. Like any good scientist, she started by researching the problem. What exactly was C8, anyway? She found out that C8, also known as APFO (ammoni-

um perfluorooctanoate), is a chemical with a chain of eight carbon atoms, which is why it's called C8. APFO is used not only in the production of Teflon but also in the manufacture of water- and stain-resistant clothing, firefighting foams, pesticides, and other products. It can also form from substances used to make grease-resistant fast-food packaging, candy wrappers, and pizza-box liners. This chemical has shown up not only in drinking water but also in the bodies of people and animals.

Then she learned something that really shocked her. This substance had been polluting her river for 50 years! And it wasn't just a local problem. Companies all over the country had been dumping the chemical in their local rivers. "Everybody has this in their blood," says Kelydra. "The average American has five parts per billion in their blood. Someone like me who lives near the factory can have up to sixty times that amount."

How much of this chemical was in the Parkersburg water supply? Nobody knew—in fact, nobody even knew of an inexpensive, reliable test that could measure the amount of APFO in water. So Kelydra decided to invent one. She wanted to create a test that was simple and didn't cost much, so that anyone in her town could analyze water coming out of their home tap. But how?

Kelydra learned that when you shake water contaminated with high amounts of APFO, the water gets foamy, and a layer of foam will rise to the top when the water settles. The more APFO in the water, the more foam there will be. The contaminated water didn't have enough APFO to make it foam, so Kelydra boiled her water sample to reduce the amount of water (through evaporation) and increase the concentration of APFO. Kelydra then shook the container and measured the height of the foam on the water surface. With this information, she could calculate the level of contamination of the original river water sample.

Layer of foam

Flask of water
contaminated by APFO

Now Kelydra had a reliable way to find out how much APFO was in the water. But she wanted to do more than that. She didn't just want to measure the problem—she wanted to solve it. So she started working on a way to remove APFO from the water. She finally succeeded by using a device called an electrolytic cell, consisting of a dry cell battery (like the kind of battery used in battery-powered toys, just bigger) and two electrodes (rods that conduct electricity). Kelydra submerged the electrodes in a flask of contaminated water. Then, in a process called electrosorption, one of the electrodes became an electrically charged wand that attracted the APFO in the water. Kelydra could then remove the rod, rinse it off, and put it back in the water to draw out more of the chemical.

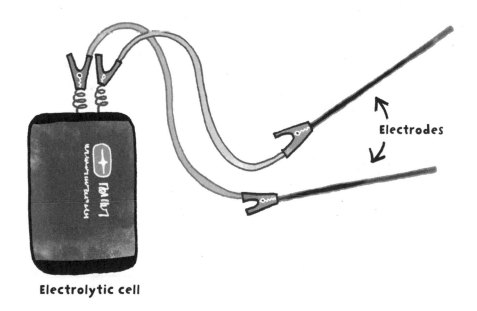

Electrolytic cell

Kelydra then added another ingredient to the flask: activated carbon. Made from charcoal, activated carbon looks like grains of black sand and is used in water filters. The carbon filtered out even more of the APFO. Kelydra repeated the electrosorption and carbon-filtering process until the water was completely free of APFO—and safe to drink.

And where did Kelydra get the high-quality electrodes she needed for the system? They were her dad's windshield wipers—minus the rubber blades! (They happened to be the perfect wand-like shape for the job.) "He wasn't terribly happy with me," she says. "I had to pay for new windshield wipers for his car."

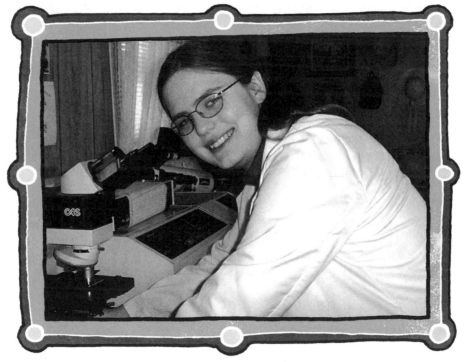

Kelydra Welcker in her lab

Using her new techniques, Kelydra developed a system that people could use to treat their own household drinking water—and she got a patent for it. The patent registration cost her $1,020.80.

How did she pay for it? "I have always picked up cans along the back-country roads and taken them to recycling. It took more than 50,000 cans to get that kind of money!" The system is being used by people in her community, and she hopes that some day it will be used more widely.

After finishing high school, Kelydra went to college, where she is studying chemistry. "I hope to expand my horizons. I'm looking at a chemical called magnesium dioxide, found in water systems. For some reason it's building up in our area, and it may cause health problems."

"Technology helped create our problems," she says, "and technology can help solve them. I want to be part of that effort."

THREE

Turning Waste into Good Business and Good Jobs

"If you have a use for something, it's no longer waste."
OMAR FREILLA
Founder, ReBuilders Source
The South Bronx, New York City

"Our first duty is to the place that raised us," Omar Freilla says. "For me, it's the South Bronx."

The South Bronx is known as the birthplace of hip-hop—the music, dance, and art movement that swept the world and made fortunes. It is also one of the poorest and most polluted places in the nation, with smog-choked freeways and smelly wastewater treatment plants. Day and night, huge trucks deliver construction waste to transfer stations, places where stuff that nobody wants is sorted, transferred to other trucks, and then taken away to distant landfills.

"We're a dumping ground," Omar explains. "All the garbage from the rest of New York City ends up here."

But like the founders of hip-hop, who thought of new ways to use old music, Omar started looking at garbage in a different way. "A lot of what people throw away is perfectly good," he says. "Building supplies are a great example. Just look at that stuff from construction sites in New York City—doors, sinks, toilets. People will buy those things. It's only called garbage because somebody threw it away."

Omar was just out of college and working for an environmental group called Sustainable South Bronx when he started thinking about how he could get this "good garbage" to people who could use it. Instead of destroying things like old windows and doors, why not clean them up and resell them? Why not hire people who live in the community to do the work? Better yet, why not make this business a "cooperative," which means that the people who work in the business own it and share the profits?

Out of this combination of practical thinking and determination to do something for the South Bronx, Omar started the first cooperative in the country dedicated to reusing construction waste.

To start his business, Omar put up flyers along the truck-jammed, trash-filled streets of his neighborhood, looking for people to work with him. "Fire Your Boss!" the flyers said, his way of letting other ambitious young people know that he was offering them a chance to work in a business they would also run, instead of working for someone else. He soon found four other dedicated workers. They rented a warehouse and started looking for donations of used materials.

They called up hardware stores, building supply distributors, and contractors, offering to haul things away from construction sites for free. Their warehouse began to fill up. A hardware store gave 2,000 gallons of paint that was still good but was being thrown away because it was past its expiration date. A distributor donated 80 new toilets from a project that had been canceled. Contractors added unwanted doors, sinks, ceiling fans—even theater seats and a giant popcorn machine!

At the beginning, not everyone understood what Omar was doing. Even his mother, who raised him to get a good education and a good job, was alarmed when he told her about his idea for the cooperative.

Omar Freilla in his South Bronx neighborhood

"She said, 'OK, show me what you are doing.' I told her we were reusing waste."

"'You're collecting garbage?' she said. 'I sacrificed so you could go to school to learn to pick up trash?'"

He laughs at the thought. "She came around eventually," he says.

In April 2008, Omar's cooperative, which he named ReBuilders Source, opened its doors for business and began selling construction supplies—at reasonable prices—to neighborhood builders and home-owners. With the help of city officials, he also began planning a new training program to help local residents learn the skills they need to get good jobs that help the environment and even start cooperatives of their own.

Omar envisions a future with a whole network of green worker co-ops in the South Bronx—cooperative businesses that will work together to reuse different kinds of construction materials. A major part will be creating businesses that deconstruct buildings instead of demolishing them. Workers will be trained to carefully take buildings apart so that things like doors, windows, and floors can be reused instead of being smashed to bits and sent off to a landfill. Deconstructing buildings this way could be a huge industry with many good jobs for people who need them.

"Think about a wooden door that you buy new. In order to produce that, someone had to cut down trees. In order to ship it across the country, someone had to pump oil out of the ground. You can avoid all that if you buy a perfectly good door that's used. And at the same time, you can reduce pollution, save money, and create jobs in communities like the South Bronx."

"If you have a use for something," Omar says, "it's no longer waste."

FOUR

Bringing Solar Power to Indian Country

"With solar energy, we can be independent."
DEBBY TEWA
Solar Electrician
Hopi Indian Reservation, Arizona

Until she was ten years old, Debby Tewa lived with her grandmother in a three-room stone house in a remote area of the Hopi Reservation in Arizona. She remembers exploring the desert with her cousins and swimming in little ponds. Like other families around them, Debby and her grandmother never had running water or a telephone, or electrical power. For heating, cooking, and lighting, they used coal, wood, and kerosene. "I didn't miss electricity then," Debby recalls. "I didn't know that I didn't have it."

Debby is a solar electrician—and a light-bringer. She brings electric light and power to some of the most isolated places on the Hopi and Navajo reservations—communities like the one where she grew up. "I can identify with the people I'm helping," she says. "I really understand their excitement when they turn on a light for the first time."

Hopi land has been home to Debby's family for many generations. It is a beautiful, dry desert environment, with three major mesas (rocky tables of land) that rise as high as 7,200 feet (nearly 2,200 meters). Surrounding the mesas are low-altitude deserts and gullies. Most people live either in the 12 traditional villages on top of the mesas or in modern communities below. The high-mesa villages are famous around the world for their culture and long history. Old Oraibi, for example, is believed to be the oldest continuously inhabited community in the United States—established more than 850 years ago, around the year 1150.

Many Hopi households are connected to the electrical grid, which means they get electricity from the power company's lines, like most city-dwellers all over the country. But several hundred households on the 1.6 million–acre (647,00-hectare) reservation are too far away from the power lines to hook into the grid.

Debby was in the fourth grade and living with her parents off the reservation when she first had electricity at home. "I liked being able to study at night and watch TV," she remembers. She started thinking about how she could help bring electricity to places like her grandmother's community.

After graduating at the top of her class from Sherman Indian High School in California, Debby returned to the Hopi Reservation, where she took a job helping other young people find summer work.

One day, a woman came to the office to recruit boys to attend trade school. "Can girls go too?" Debby asked. When the woman said yes, Debby jumped at the chance.

"We could choose electricity or plumbing," Debby remembers. "At first, I chose plumbing because I was scared of electricity. Then a couple of Hopi classmates wanted me to come over to electricity. They promised they would help me out if I did. And sure enough, they did help." Later, she got to help them when they worked together on jobs. "I'm lucky because I've always had a lot of support for what I'm doing."

Debby's next big opportunity came in 1987, when The Hopi Foundation, created by Hopi people to improve life on the reservation, started an organization called Native Sun. The idea was to bring energy to isolated Hopi communities in a way that would fit in with their traditional way of life. Solar energy seemed like a perfect solution. It didn't cause the pollution and health problems that coal-powered plants did. It was silent, it was easy to install, and it required very little maintenance. Best of

Debby and her crew installing solar panels

37

all, since the energy was coming from the sun, it was "renewable" energy, meaning the supply wouldn't get used up.

Solar power would also enable Hopi households to be "energy independent," because they wouldn't have to rely on energy from power companies outside their land. To spread the word about solar energy, The Hopi Foundation recruited several members of the tribe who could speak the Hopi language. One of them was Debby Tewa.

Part of Debby's job was to teach people about solar energy—how to choose the right solar electric system, how to use it, and how to take care of it. "I wanted them to feel that it was theirs." But first she had to get people interested.

Solar panels are made of many solar cells. When sunlight strikes the solar cells, the energy causes electrons in the cells' atoms to break free from the nuclei they orbit. These free electrons then flow into an electric current. Electricity is stored in batteries connected to the solar panels, so the system still works at night and on cloudy days.

Debby set up demonstration solar power systems in three villages on the mesas. People came to see how solar panels could be wired into their houses so they could have electricity. A 90-year-old woman was amazed that she could flick a switch and light would come on. A seamstress could use an electric sewing machine. Kids could do schoolwork and watch TV at night. And they didn't have to pay for the new system all at once, because Native Sun offered loans to their customers.

When people wanted to try it out, Debby loaned them a small trailer-mounted system for a week. This helped them decide how large a system they wanted, and then Debby would drive out and install it.

Debby explaining how a
solar panel works

She would strap on her tool belt, climb up a ladder onto the roof, and go to work. Sometimes she would be on top of a 200-year-old stone house, looking out over a hundred miles of low desert and high mesas. In the next few years, Debby installed more than 300 solar panels on Hopi houses, and people on the reservation started calling her "Solar Debby." She also installed solar panels on the neighboring Navajo Reservation and trained other electricians, especially women, in places as far away as Ecuador in South America.

Debby has four solar panels on her own house on the reservation. That's enough for lights and TV. "It's not like the power lines bring," she says, "but it's enough."

For people like Debby's aunt and her aunt's 90-year-old neighbor, who had never had electricity before, solar power has made a life-changing difference. They no longer have to read by the light of a propane lamp. But best of all, they know that they have control over their own electricity.

"When you get your own solar electrical system, it's yours," Debby explains. "You're not dependent on a power company. With solar energy, we can be independent."

Debby Tewa

FIVE

Speaking Out to a Big Oil Company

"If you don't tell people the problem, how can you expect them to solve it?"

MARGIE RICHARD

Activist and Former Middle School Teacher
Old Diamond, Louisiana

In 2001, Margie Richard traveled to a city called The Hague, in the Netherlands, to attend a board of directors meeting for one of the most powerful oil companies in the world. She was holding on to a valuable piece of evidence—a plastic bucket containing a bag of contaminated air from her hometown in Louisiana.

She was the last speaker from the floor. A small, determined woman, she edged her way through the crowd until she was facing a row of the company's leaders. She looked straight at them and held up her bucket.

"Would you want your children to breathe this air?"

There was laughter from the crowd. The men looked puzzled. "What's this about?" one of them asked.

"The people of my community have to breathe polluted air from your factory day and night. I've come across the world to ask if you will help us move to a safer place." One of the speakers said he would look into it.

After the meeting, Margie found the man in the hall and insisted on telling him her story—how the fumes from his company's plant were poisoning people in Old Diamond, how they had been getting rare forms of cancer, and how they had been trying for 13 years to get the company to help them move.

The man listened. He was an oilman, a company man, but he was also a father. And he didn't want bad publicity for his company. He said he would see what he could do.

Margie's town, Old Diamond, Louisiana, was a close-knit African American community 25 miles (40 kilometers) west of New Orleans on the banks of the Mississippi River. Sandwiched between a giant oil refinery and a chemical plant, its residents were subject to some of the worst industrial pollution in the country.

Old Diamond had once been part of a plantation that was divided up at the end of the Civil War. Some of the rich farmland was purchased by former slaves. Margie's grandfather had owned a thriving farm where he grew corn, lettuce, and cantaloupes.

Then, in 1953, when Margie was nine, her family was pressured to sell their land to the oil company next door. The company wanted to build a new plant to manufacture petrochemicals (chemicals like pesticides and fertilizers made from the leftovers of the oil-refining process). African Americans in the South had few civil rights in those years, so it would have been difficult to fight back. Everyone in Old Diamond had to move to a much smaller piece of land—right up against the fence line of the new petrochemical plant.

Emissions from the factory's smokestacks turned the air into a haze of chemicals. "Twelve-thirty at night, that smoke would come out," Margie recalls. "Six-thirty in the morning, it was still there, making us sick."

There were other dangers, too. In 1973, a 16-year-old boy was mowing the lawn when a spark from his lawnmower ignited gas that had leaked from a pipeline. The explosion killed him and his elderly neighbor. Margie was grown by that time and was teaching school. But like everybody else in Old Diamond, she was scared. "I started sleeping in my clothes, so I could jump up and run for my life if I had to."

Most of the people in Old Diamond wanted to move—and they wanted the oil company to pay for it. But how could they make one of the most powerful companies in the world listen to them? Margie remembers going to a meeting of elder churchwomen to decide what to do. The minute she walked in, they looked up. "There she is," one of them said. "We choose you to be our leader."

"How could I say no," Margie says, "when I cared about them so much?"

Margie organized a group of concerned citizens to deal with the problem. They met every week in members' houses, often in

Margie Richard

Margie's trailer, to discuss and write down their concerns. At the top of the list was a demand for relocation.

The group filed a lawsuit against the oil company. All of them had relatives or friends who they believed had been made sick or had died because of long-term exposure to emissions from the oil refinery and chemical plant. Margie's sister had died at age 43 of sarcoidosis, a rare lung disease. "In the end she had no lungs," Margie remembers. "She had to breathe pure oxygen from a tank."

The lawsuit failed. Even though people were getting sick, the oil company said that it wasn't their fault. Where was the proof?

Margie was bitterly disappointed. Some of her supporters turned away, saying that she was foolish to think she could win against such a powerful opponent. But Margie continued speaking out. Over time, people from across the country—scientists, environmentalists, activists, lawyers—began coming to her trailer with offers of help.

In 1998, Denny Larson, an activist from California, arrived with a way to prove that Old Diamond air contained dangerous chemicals. Denny brought an ordinary bucket that had a special plastic bag inside with a hose and pump, so that people could take samples of the bad air and send them to a lab to be tested. The lab reports confirmed that the air contained a dangerous mix of chemicals, including methyl ethyl ketone, which is an explosive, and carbon disulfide, a chemical that attacks the nervous system. Here was the evidence Margie was looking for. It was one of these buckets that she took to the meeting in The Hague.

In 2001, two weeks after Margie returned from that meeting, a big car pulled up in front of her trailer. It was a warm, sunny day. The air didn't smell too bad. The man in the car said, "Hello, are you Margie Richard? I just stopped by for a chat." He was one of the European managers of the company, and he wanted to know the extent of the problem. There didn't seem to be a problem that he could see.

Suddenly, flames exploded from one of the plant's smokestacks. The man started to cough. He rubbed his eyes. "What's that?"

Margie smiled. How many times had she and her supporters told the company the air was dangerous in Old Diamond?

Finally, on March 4, 2002, the oil company began talking to Margie and her group about relocation. Four months later, the oil company agreed to buy the homes of everyone who wanted to move—almost all of the nearly 400 residents—and pay them enough to buy another house in a safe location. After 14 years of struggle, Margie and her supporters had won!

This victory of a small, poor, African American community against one of the most powerful companies in the world was an inspiration to other communities in the United States and throughout the world. Today, Margie travels all over the world to help other communities get fair treatment from big oil companies. Everywhere she goes, she speaks out about injustice. "I get accused of talking too much," she says, "but if you don't tell people the problem, how can you expect them to solve it?"

SIX

Inventing Eco-Machines

"We must work with nature instead of fighting it."
JOHN TODD
Inventor, Engineer, and Designer
Woods Hole, Massachusetts

John Todd was one of those kids who didn't like school. But he did like nature—and he liked inventing things.

As a child, growing up in Canada, he loved to explore the woods around his house, observing how nature solved problems. A dirty stream, for example, often became clear after flowing through plants and along rocks where tiny creatures lived. When he got older, John started to wonder if this same process could be used to clean up the messes that people were making.

After studying agriculture, tropical medicine, fisheries, and ocean-ography in college, John went back to observing nature directly and asking all kinds of questions. Why is it that certain plants can trap harm-ful bacteria? Which kinds of tiny fish can eat cancer-causing chemicals? With the right combination of animals and plants, he figured, maybe he

could clean up waste the way nature did. He decided to build what he would later call an "eco-machine."

He tried his first experiment at a landfill on Cape Cod, Massachusetts, near the laboratory where he worked. The task he set for himself was to decontaminate a sample of sewer sludge from the landfill. First, he constructed a series of clear fiberglass tanks connected to each other— not in a straight line, but more like the twists and turns of a river. Then he went around to local ponds, streams, wetlands, even wet places in the woods, and brought back plant and animal specimens. He placed the specimens in the tanks and waited. Little by little, all these different kinds of life got used to one another and formed their own ecosystem, which means their own way of living together. Finally, after a few weeks, John added the sludge from the landfill and waited to see what would happen.

He was amazed at the results. The plants and animals in the eco-machine recognized the sewage sludge as food—and began to eat it! Within weeks, the sewage had all been digested by the eco-machine, and all that was left was pure water.

How did John know how to build his eco-machine, and what to put in it? He says his success was "one-third chemistry, one-third ecology, and one-third serendipity"—that means it was partly knowing about the chemical makeup of things, partly knowing how the living parts of an environment fit together, and partly good luck.

"Ecological design" is the name John gives to what he does. "Life on Earth is kind of a bin of spare parts for the inventor," he says. "You put organisms in new relationships and observe what's happening. Then you let these new systems develop their own ways to self-repair."

John's first chance to try out his ideas with kids came when a school in Canada contacted him about recycling its sewage. Could he build an eco-machine that would purify human waste and also be educational for the students? And could he make it look really nice—like a giant water sculpture that would fit in the main hall of the school? The answer was yes.

John Todd

He began by constructing a series of 17 interconnected glass tanks that coiled down like a giant snail, starting with a tank that was 14 feet (43 meters) tall and ending with a tank that was 4 feet (1.2 meters) tall. Then he went looking for the plants and animals to put into his machine. Sometimes students went with him to ponds and streams near the school. He filled the tallest tank with algae, the next few tanks with rooted aquatic plants, and the shortest tanks—easiest for the students to view—with tiny clams, snails, and fish. Finally, he connected his machine to the school toilets and told the kids to start flushing!

The raw sewage was first digested by microorganisms (in non-transparent pipes, so no one had to look at poop!). Next, the partially purified sewage was pumped up to the highest of the 17 glass tanks, and the students watched it flow from tank to tank, becoming cleaner and cleaner as the impurities were eaten by the algae, the bacteria, and the fish and snails. The almost clean water that flowed out of the last tank was pumped through a marsh outside the school, collected in a pond, and finally recycled back to the toilets.

"Technically, at that point, the water was clean enough for drinking," John says, "but nobody wants to think about drinking water that originally came from the toilet."

Over the years, John has taken on bigger and bigger jobs. In a project sponsored by the United States Environmental Protection Agency, John developed a greenhouse-like facility that treated sewage from 1,600 homes in South Burlington, Vermont. In the town's Municipal Treatment Plant, he explains, "we substituted nature's wisdom for heavy-duty engineering, chemicals, and massive amounts of energy. In almost any other sewage plant, you would have been overwhelmed by the stink. But at South Burlington, there was hardly any smell at all."

The eco-machine John designed to clean toilet water for a Canadian school

In Fuzhou, a crowded city in southeast China, a complicated network of sewage canals runs through the city center before emptying into a nearby river. The water in the 50 miles (80 kilometers) of canals is gray and lifeless, with all kinds of garbage floating in it. The stench, according to John, is "beyond reason."

A floating eco-machine that cleans canal water in Fuzhou, China

But on a tiny section of Fuzhou's canals—just 650 yards (600 meters)—something amazing is happening. A floating eco-machine resembling a beautiful botanical garden is restoring the water to health. At work in the eco-machine are 100,000 plants, three species of Chinese carp, and two strains of bacteria. The plants grow on two long racks with a walkway down the center. Below the surface, bacteria that digest sludge and grease are piped into the system and blowers pump air into the canal to maintain high levels of oxygen in the water.

After just one year of operation, the water in the canal beside the eco-machine is much cleaner, no longer stinks, and contains abundant fish. Neighbors are seeing butterflies and birds by their canal for the first time in their lives.

John's dream project for the future is to help heal the Appalachian mountain region of West Virginia and Kentucky, an area that has been devastated by poverty and by mountaintop removal mining. He plans to treat toxic mining waste, rebuild the soil, develop renewable energies, such as solar and wind power—and make sure that this transformation also brings good, environmentally based jobs to the people who live there.

"The way to change the world," John says, "is to work with nature instead of fighting it."

SEVEN

Recycling Electronic Waste

"Today's technology should not become
tomorrow's toxic trash."

ALEX LIN

Teenager Who Helped Write Rhode Island's E-Waste Law
Westerly, Rhode Island

When Alex Lin was 11 years old, he read an alarming article in the newspaper about electronic trash, known as e-waste. The article said that people were dumping their e-waste in places it should never go. They were burying old computers in backyards, throwing TVs into streams, and tossing cell phones in the garbage. This was dangerous, the article said, because e-waste contains poisonous chemicals and toxic metals like mercury and lead. These harmful substances can leak into the environment, getting into crops, animals, water supplies—and people.

"I was really worried," Alex remembers. "Just think about it. You know those toys that have been recalled because they contain tiny

amounts of lead that could be dangerous to children? Well, consider this: each CRT (cathode ray tube) monitor contains four to eight pounds (nearly two to four kilograms) of lead."

Alex showed the article to a few of his classmates. They were worried too. "What if it's happening here? We could be poisoning the environment and not even know it."

"Maybe we can help," Alex said. "I think we should make this our next project for WIN."

WIN was the Westerly Innovations Network, named for their town of Westerly, Rhode Island. Two years before, Alex, then nine years old, and six of his buddies had formed the organization to help solve community problems. All of them were part of a national program that teaches kids to become community leaders. Alex's father is a coach with WIN. "He makes sure that we plan each project in a practical way," says Alex.

But what could they do about this problem with e-waste? How would they even start?

"The first thing we did," Alex says, "was to learn more about the problem." Alex and his friends spent several weeks gathering information about the chemicals in e-waste and their effects on humans. They learned how to dispose of e-waste properly and how it could be recycled. "Then," he says, "we had to find out what the situation was in our town. So we sent out a survey."

What they found amazed them: Of the people who answered the survey, only one in eight even knew what e-waste was, let alone how

Alex Lin, age 14

to properly dispose of it. One man had dug a huge hole in his backyard and dumped about 50 old Mac computers inside it. "It was a business he had," Alex says. "He bought up old computers, took the valuable parts he could resell, and then dumped everything else. He didn't see anything wrong with that."

Alex and his friends went into action. They advertised in the local newspaper and distributed notices to students, asking residents to bring their unwanted electronics to the school parking lot. The drive lasted two days, and they collected over 21,000 pounds (over 9,500 kilograms) of e-waste, including the school system's obsolete computers, which were being stored in an old school bus.

The next step was to set up a permanent e-waste drop-off center for the town and to find a responsible company to recycle the waste. That was when Alex and his friends learned another scary fact about e-waste—some irresponsible recycling companies don't break down the e-waste and dispose of it safely themselves. Instead, they ship it overseas to countries such as China and Nigeria, where local environmental laws are not enforced and kids their age work at picking apart and burning e-waste (to get at the valuable metals) with no masks or other kinds of protection. After a while, these kids get very sick. "We checked carefully online to make sure the company we chose didn't do this," Alex says.

After setting up the e-waste drop-off center, Alex's team began to think about how to reuse some of the old computers so they wouldn't have to be recycled. "In our research, we'd learned that reusing is the best way to deal with electronic devices that people don't want anymore," Alex says. "That's because you can save energy and resources. Reusing is seven times more efficient than recycling. If we could refurbish computers ourselves and distribute them to students who didn't have their own, we could help students in our area and protect the environment at the same time."

Alex (age 11) and the WIN team collecting e-waste

Alex persuaded his school to start teaching students how to refurbish donated computers. These students were able to collect, restore, and distribute 260 computers to kids who needed them. Alex

is especially proud of this part of his project. He was thanked on video by the mother of one of the students who got a free computer. "I couldn't afford to buy a computer for my daughter, so she always had to go to the library to do her homework. Now, thanks to Alex and his group, she can do her homework at home."

Alex and his team refurbishing old computers

For a lasting solution to e-waste, the drop-off center wasn't enough. Laws would have to be passed. In 2005, Alex and his team met with state representatives who were pushing for an e-waste bill in Rhode Island. Their bill was very complicated—among other things, it required companies that manufactured or sold electronics to take back e-waste. The bill did not pass. Then, in the spring of 2006, Alex testified at the state house in favor of a new e-waste bill that would simply forbid the dumping of e-waste. He and other support-ers talked to legislators, made slide presentations, and collected more than 370 signatures. And this time, they won! The bill became law on

July 8, 2006, making Rhode Island the fourth state in the nation to create legislation for the safe disposal of e-waste.

Since e-waste is a global problem, Alex and his friends are spreading their project internationally. With the help of business sponsors, they now have WIN teams in Mexico and three African countries. In 2007, they shipped a full refurbished media center—including ten computers, a printer, a scanning and copying machine, a projector, and a projection screen—to a school in Mexico City. During spring break, they visited the school and made presentations to help educate the students about e-waste. They have also shipped two refurbished media centers to Africa—one to an Internet café in Cameroon and one to a cultural center in Nigeria.

Because of the work of people like Alex and his team, more and more people are getting the message about safe disposal of e-waste. As Alex says, "Today's technology should not become tomorrow's toxic trash."

EIGHT

Saving West Virginia's Oldest Mountains

"It makes a lot more sense to build windmills
than to blow up mountains."

JULIA "JUDY" BONDS

Community Activist, Coal River Mountain Watch
Whitesville, West Virginia

Julia Bonds is proud to be a coal miner's daughter. She remembers her father going deep into the earth to chip away at the veins of coal. "Most of the men were miners back then," she recalls. "And the coal they mined made energy for people all over America."

Mining was hard, dangerous work. "We were always scared when he was down there that he might never come back up." The job didn't pay very much either. Miners were poor. But in spite of the dangers and the poverty, Julia loved her town, Marfork Hollow, West Virginia, where six generations of her family had been born and raised. "We felt safe and protected in our little valley with the mountains all around."

But by the time Julia became a grandmother in the 1980s, everything was beginning to change. The coal companies decided that it cost too much to send men down into the mines, or even to dig down from the surface to reach the veins of coal. Instead, they began to blast the tops right off the mountains to get directly at the coal. They called this new way of doing things "mountaintop removal mining."

Every step of mountaintop removal mining is a disaster for the environment. First, the mountain is cleared of all vegetation, including the valuable hardwood trees and fertile topsoil, which are all pushed into the valley below. Then holes are drilled in the mountain and filled with explosives. "They put in 3 million pounds (1.3 million kilograms) of dynamite every day," Julia says, "except for Sunday."

After the blast is set off, the rubble, called "overburden," is picked up by giant machines and dropped into the valley below, creating "valley fills" that can be a mile wide and hundreds of feet high. These valley fills bury mountain streams, and as they settle they sometimes collapse in heavy rains.

When the mountaintop is gone, the coal is scooped up with heavy machinery and washed in a mix of water and chemicals to separate the coal from the rock and dirt. The coal is loaded into trucks or trains that speed down the mountain on their way to coal-fired power plants up and down the East Coast. What's left behind is a gooey, toxic mix of coal dust, chemicals, and water, called "sludge." And where is it stored?

In hundreds of open ponds called "impoundments," which are held in place by earthen dams.

Julia is very concerned about the safety of these dams. "There's a 2.8 billion-gallon (10.6 billion liter) sludge dam sitting directly above Marsh Fork Elementary School, and we can see that it's leaking all over the face of it." She worries about what could happen if that dam gives way when the children are in school. "A few years back," she says, "a dam like this collapsed and 147 people drowned."

She remembers the string of events that warned her about the dangers of mountaintop removal mining. "The first thing was all the people above us moving out—and then the bears coming down out of the mountains because they'd lost their habitat. There was coal dust over everything. It had kind of an orange color to it from the chemicals. Then the creek turned black, above where we got our drinking water. Then the blasting, and the noise from the train taking the coal out. It was a nightmare—like nine years living in a war zone."

Mountaintop removal mining has destroyed more than 470 mountains in Appalachia

Julia Bonds

The day finally came in 1998 when she knew she had to take action. She was wading in a favorite stream above her house with her grandson, when he bent over and scooped up a bunch of dead fish. "Grandma, what happened to these fish?" he asked. Julia says her heart just about stopped beating. "Honey," she told him, "these fish were poisoned." In that moment, she realized that mountaintop removal mining was stealing the earth away from the children. She had to help take it back.

Julia joined Coal River Mountain Watch, a citizens' group dedicated to protecting Appalachia and its people from the ravages of mountaintop removal mining. Working from a small storefront, she was soon devoting 90 hours a week to talking with people throughout the coal mining areas, telling them how they could fight back. They could report leaking sludge dams or illegal blasting or overloaded coal trucks going dangerously fast on the mountain roads.

A few neighbors did call in complaints, but others were afraid of what could happen to them if they spoke out against the powerful coal companies. You could lose your job or your house. Julia's grandson is one of the very few young people in the region who has joined her protests against mountaintop removal mining. She worries about him constantly. Julia herself has received death threats. "You have to understand that this is not like the rest of the U.S.A.," Julia explains. "Coal is king here, and he rules with an iron fist."

Nevertheless, Julia was able to win some important victories. In 2004, a bulldozer, operating illegally at 2:30 a.m., dislodged a boulder that rolled down the mountain and crashed into the bedroom of a sleeping child, killing him instantly. Julia and other activists organized a protest march. As a result of their action, the state mining board pressured the coal companies to stop illegal nighttime operations. After overloaded coal trucks rushing down the mountains had killed several children and damaged the mountain roads, Julia worked with the United Mineworkers Union to ban overloaded coal trucks.

Her courage and effectiveness began to gain national attention—and support. In 2003, Julia won the Goldman Environmental Prize (the biggest prize in the environmental world) and started bringing in journalists, politicians, and other activists to show them the devastation caused by mountaintop removal mining. From the air, Julia's visitors could see that great sections of West Virginia now look like the surface of the moon. More than 470 mountains and thousands of mountain streams are gone forever. A popular local bumper sticker reads, "I have been to the mountaintop, but it wasn't there."

Julia also started taking her message to colleges across the country. "Do you know where you get your electricity from?" she asked the students. "It's amazing how many people don't know." She went on to explain that half the electricity in the United States comes from coal-fired power plants, and that many of these power plants use coal from mountaintop removal mining. Burning this coal pollutes the air and water and gives off large amounts of greenhouse gases, which contribute to climate change.

Beginning in 2005, Julia and other activists put out a call for young people to come to Appalachia to help fight mountaintop removal mining. The program, called Mountain Justice Summer, brings hundreds of young volunteers to coal communities all over the mountains where they help to test water samples, research new permit applications by the mining companies, and interview local people to document mining company abuses.

Twenty-two-year-old Jen Jackson, horrified by the stories she heard about "fish being cut open, appearing normal from the outside but black as coal on the inside," helped get the coal companies to deliver clean water to communities whose wells had been contaminated with mining sludge. Geography student Jen Osha, 26, is working with residents of Big Coal River Valley to map the areas of proposed new mines. For the first time ever, before a mining permit is approved, people will be able to see how that mine could affect their homes, creeks, and hunting and fishing grounds. Ivan Stiefel, 22, is working with residents to force officials to move Marsh Fork Elementary School to a safe place away from the sludge dam. He has also created a new organization, Mountain Justice Spring Break, to bring college students to help during their schools' spring break.

National attention from the media, the public, and environmental organizations has helped expose the injustices of mountaintop removal mining—and has drawn expert legal help to Julia and other activists. "We've slowed down the mining companies in getting new permits," Julia says, "and we're pressing forward with legislation and lawsuits. We have a bill in Congress now that would make it illegal to dump mining waste into our mountain streams. We're also suing the mining companies to make them stop blowing up our mountains."

Julia's vision for the future? To gradually replace coal mining with renewable energy. She's working to start a wind farm, one of the largest in the eastern United States, and she's counting on young people to help build and run it. "There's a lot of wind up there on those mountain ridges," she says. "It makes a lot more sense to build windmills than to blow up mountains."

NINE

Fighting the Enemies of the Environment

"This is the most important fight of my life—and I need all the children to be on my team."

EL HIJO DEL SANTO ("SON OF THE SAINT")

Champion Masked Wrestler
Mexico City, Mexico

In 2007, a famous wrestler wearing a silver mask left the ring in Mexico City and headed north. His name: El Hijo del Santo—"Santo" for short. His mission: to fight the Enemies of the Environment. His destination: the border city of Tijuana, Mexico.

In Tijuana, he drove up a steep canyon to meet with a group of kids at their school. The kids could hardly believe that one of the most popular sports stars in Mexico had come to their community. They'd seen him on TV, always fighting the bad guys, always wearing his silver mask. Why was he here?

"I want you to help me fight pollution," Santo said.

The Tijuana River, which flows through their community, was badly polluted, he explained. Playing in the river could make them sick.

Why was the river so polluted? Partly, it was because of untreated sewage and pollution from factories. Another reason was that people were dumping trash in it. "I want you to throw trash in the trash bins and not in the river," he said. "Santo is fighting to keep the river clean, but he can't do it alone. He needs the help of all the children. Are you with me? Will you be on my team?"

The kids raised their fists and shouted, "We're with you, Santo!"

Santo is a star of *lucha libre* ("free fighting"), a theatrical style of wrestling that is the second most popular sport in Mexico (after soccer). The fighters wear colorful masks and flashy costumes representing heroes and villains. "Our fights are like the struggle between good and evil," Santo explains. "I'm one of the good guys."

After years of a successful wrestling career, Santo was listening to the radio one day when he heard an announcement by an environmental group called WiLDCOAST, or in Spanish COSTASALVAjE. "We're fighting to protect the wild coastline on both sides of the U.S.-Mexico border," the announcer explained. "We're looking for a famous personality who cares about the environment and who can help us get our message across." Santo was interested. Santo had hundreds of thousands of fans in Mexico and the United States, and he wanted to use his popularity for a new cause. In the ring, he was a hero. This was his chance to be a hero outside the ring, too. He agreed to volunteer for a year.

Ben McCue, a young environmentalist in charge of the clean water campaign for WiLDCOAST, accompanied Santo as he met with the kids in Tijuana. "Santo really got their attention," Ben says. "He sat down and talked to them about simple things that they could do to keep the river cleaner and protect themselves and their pets. They're going to remember what he says for a long time—and get their families involved, too."

Kids from Tijuana, Mexico, wearing masks of popular wrestling stars

After his visit to the school, Santo inspected the site of a new waste-water treatment plant that WiLDCOAST is proposing to build for the school and 50 households. "The way it is now," Ben explains, "when it rains, household waste overflows into the Tijuana River and out to the ocean on the U.S. side of the border. This treatment plant will help prevent that."

The kids from San Ignacio Lagoon, Mexico, let Santo know that they're on his team and want to help clean up the environment

Santo also watched kids making special paving stones called "pervious pavers," which will be used to pave the dirt streets in their community. Rainwater can pass right through pervious pavers into the earth, instead of running off and causing floods. Santo told the kids how important this work was and how proud he was of them. He announced that he would help support this project by donating all the money from a benefit fight at the big arena in downtown Tijuana.

As Santo talked to kids and walked around the community, he was filmed by a TV crew. When the story was broadcast, thousands of people in the United States and Mexico saw how important it was to clean up the Tijuana River. "The TV coverage helped focus public attention on the issue," Ben says. It may have also helped speed up some important changes. Shortly after Santo's tour, the U.S. Congress decided to fund an upgrade to the wastewater treatment plant on the U.S. side of the border, and on the Mexican side the city of Tijuana opened a new, larger wastewater treatment plant.

After leaving Tijuana, Santo traveled to a remote nesting site for sea turtles on the Gulf of Mexico. A TV unit from the BBC World News went with him. People all over the world saw Santo watching over a group of baby turtles as they made their way to the sea. He explained that sea turtles have lived on Earth for more than 150 million years. "They go back to the days of the dinosaurs," he said. "It is important to protect them."

Later, Santo traveled to San Ignacio Lagoon, on Mexico's Pacific coast, a birthing place for the Pacific gray whale. On a boat in the lagoon, camera operators from five major Latin American networks filmed Santo in his silver mask as he reached out to pet a huge Pacific gray whale. San Ignacio Lagoon is one of the few places on Earth where these whales give birth. The warm waters of the lagoon help the baby whales survive until they develop blubber (whale fat) to protect them from the colder water of the open ocean.

Santo explained to his television audience that companies want to mine salt and drill for oil and gas here—and to build big tourist resorts. If they do, the development would pollute the lagoon and possibly destroy the Pacific gray whale birthing ground. Santo asked his audience to support the work of WiLDCOAST as well as other groups in Mexico and the United States that are working to protect the lagoon. Some, like the NRDC (Natural Resources Defense Council), are keeping industry out by purchasing the rights to the land around the lagoon so others can't build on it. Others are helping local people make money through farming or whale-watching tours, so they won't have to sell their land.

When Santo visited the school near the lagoon, he told the kids that their lagoon was one of the most beautiful places in the world. Many of them didn't know that, because they'd never traveled anywhere else. "Will you help me?" he asked them. "Will you talk to your families about how important it is to protect the lagoon? Are you with me?" Like the kids in Tijuana, they answered, "We're with you, Santo!"

Santo's televised campaign against the Enemies of the Environment brought international attention to the urgent need to protect San Ignacio Lagoon—and it attracted funding to help pay for that protection. The television coverage also gave credit to the kids and their families for helping to protect the lagoon, which was very important to Santo.

El Hijo del Santo holds a baby
sea turtle about to hatch

When Santo completed the first year of his work, 7,000 fans watched him accept a "Hero of the Environment" award at the Monterey Bay Aquarium in California. He was so moved that he volunteered for another year. "This is the most important fight of my life," he told his audience, "and I need all the children to be on my team."

81

TEN

Protecting the Louisiana Wetlands

"I want all my students to feel like heroes."
BARRY GUILLOT
Middle School Science Teacher
Destrehan, Louisiana

On June 1, 2005, science teacher Barry Guillot and 25 of his students gave a presentation in the historic French Quarter of New Orleans. Wearing bright orange life jackets, the students lined second-floor balconies and unrolled sea-blue tarps that reached down to the street, dramatically illustrating how high the floodwaters could rise if a hurricane hit the city dead on. The students were members of LaBranche Wetland Watchers, an organization that Barry started. They were warning the public that if the health of the wetlands around the city continued to be ignored, there could be a catastrophe.

Barry remembers the comment of a man passing in the street. "We all know it's possible, but it's not really going to happen."

But it did happen. Three months later, Hurricane Katrina hit New Orleans. It was the most destructive hurricane in the city's history. The French Quarter, where the students had delivered their warning, received relatively mild damage. But in the lower-lying areas of the city, the floods were devastating and people lost everything—in some cases, even their lives.

Barry Guillot

The disaster brought home the importance of wetlands to the city.

Wetlands are fresh-water marshes, swamps, and bogs—any land area that is covered with water for some part of the year. A marsh is like a prairie with water, whereas swamps and bogs have trees and are more like forests with water. Bayous are also part of wetlands—they're like small rivers through wet ground. When a storm comes, the wetlands act like sponges to absorb water that would flood the city. The trees serve as barriers to slow down winds so there isn't so much damage. "As we lose our wetlands around New Orleans, we don't have the protection from hurricanes that we used to have," Barry explains.

In the past, these wetlands were seen as a problem for cargo ships and oil tankers. They had to sail up the Mississippi River, which curves around the wetlands, to reach New Orleans from the Gulf of Mexico. To save time and money, engineers dug shipping channels directly from the Gulf of Mexico to New Orleans, right through the wetlands. The biggest of these channels was nicknamed "Mr. Go" (for Mississippi River Gulf Outlet). Cargo ships and tankers could now get to the city much faster—but so could hurricanes. They raced up these new shipping channels from the Gulf in a "storm surge," unleashing strong winds and heavy rains on the city.

Saltwater from the Gulf was coming in, too, which caused the loss of still more wetlands. When a wetland area becomes too salty, the salt kills the freshwater plants that hold the soil together, and the land gets washed away.

Louisiana's wetlands are disappearing very quickly. An area the size of a football field gets washed away every 35 minutes. "Imagine if the New Orleans Saints, our football team, were playing on a field that was actually wetlands," Barry says. "By halftime, that football field would be gone, and there would be water in its place."

Growing up in Terrytown, Louisiana, across the Mississippi River from New Orleans, Barry loved exploring the wetlands with his friends. When he became a middle school science teacher, he wanted his kids to learn about the wetlands. He wanted to teach them not only in the classroom but outdoors, and to show them how to help their community at the same time.

In 1998, he founded the LaBranche Wetland Watchers Service-Learning Project, "adopting" a small part of LaBranche Wetlands near their school. The area had suffered from soil loss, high salt-water levels, and trash that people dumped there. What could a science teacher and a group of middle school students possibly do to help?

They began by exploring "their wetlands," with the help of university scientists and local people who had grown up in the area. Kids learned to test water quality, organize group cleanups, plant trees to hold the soil in place, and help build cement barriers to keep saltwater out.

Barry remembers an early outing with 35 students. "Now you have to become the experts," he told them. Based on what they'd learned, he asked what they wanted to do first. "Plant trees," they answered. But how could they afford it? "I hooked up with the U.S. Department of Agriculture," Barry explains. "They were so amazed that the students wanted to do this that they donated the trees."

The first trees they planted had name tags. When former students come to visit, they ask, "Mr. Guillot, how's my tree doing?" Those first cypress trees are part of a network of new trees helping to anchor the wetlands. "We have our own tree yard now where we grow a thousand seedling trees each year," Barry says proudly.

Barry's students planting trees
to protect the wetlands

Wetland Watchers activities are tied to academic subjects. Water-quality monitoring, for example, teaches students to use graphs to compare data from different time periods—part of the math curriculum. After Hurricane Katrina, the salinity (amount of salt in the water) was four times as high as before. Students made graphs to show that. As part of English composition, they wrote about seeing jellyfish, which had never come that far before because jellyfish live only in salty water.

"We learn a lot more than we would just sitting behind a desk with a book, because you're out there and you're getting all filthy and muddy and having fun as you learn," says Kurt, a seventh grader.

Every week, Barry brings a different animal into the classroom, including many from the wetlands. "Alligators are big-time favorites, along with turtles and amphiumas"—giant salamanders that look like eels. "But the Louisiana pine snake is the superstar. It's one of the rarest snakes in North America!"

More than a thousand students participate in Wetland Watchers activities every year, learning to become community leaders: They host weekend community trash cleanups and tree plantings and lead wetlands trips for younger students. Over the years, Barry says, his students have talked to more than 300,000 people across Louisiana about the importance of wetlands.

The Wetland Watchers have been so successful that the local government donated 28 acres of wetlands to their project, including the small tract that they started with. The official name of the new area is Wetland Watchers Park.

"We're building an outdoor classroom that all the schools can use and working on plans for more than a mile of wooden board-walk nature trails," Barry says. The students are creating all the guide material for the trails—stories about people who lived there long ago, descriptions of wetlands plants and animals, and information about how to help take care of the wetlands.

Students measuring and recording water salinity

Barry is very proud of his students. "It's amazing what middle school kids can accomplish when they get the chance," he says. One of his seventh graders wrote, "If the animals and plants could talk, I think they would say we're their heroes. That's the way I feel when we do our work in the wetlands."

That meant a lot to Barry. "I want all my students to feel like heroes."

ELEVEN

Saving the Porcupine River Caribou

"If you drill for oil here, you will be drilling into the heart of our people."

SARAH JAMES

Spokesperson, Gwich'in Indian People of Alaska and Canada
Arctic Village, Alaska

Sarah James remembers waking up as a child to the sounds of the Porcupine River caribou herd passing by her cabin. She remembers snorts and sighs and the particular clicking sound made by thousands of caribou feet. "We were happy," she says, "because we knew we were going to eat well."

Sarah's father hunted the caribou for its meat, which fed her family, and for the hides, which provided clothing and shelter. The bones and antlers were made into tools, tableware, and crafts. Nothing was wasted. "We call ourselves Caribou People," Sarah explains. "Caribou is not just what we eat: It is our clothing, our dances, our songs. It is who we are."

The Porcupine River caribou herd has been central to the culture of the Gwich'in people of Alaska and Canada for 20,000 years. Every year, this vast herd—more than 110,000 animals—travels thousands of miles from Canada's Porcupine River region to the coastal plain of the Arctic National Wildlife Refuge in Alaska, by the Arctic Ocean, where the females give birth to their young.

Caribou are members of the reindeer family. They are the only deer species in which both males and females grow antlers. The antlers, which are shed every year, have a long, sweeping main beam, up to 5 feet (1.5 meters) across.

The 15 widely separated Gwich'in villages are located along the caribou migration route across parts of Alaska and Canada's Yukon and Northwest Territories. Nine thousand people live in these villages, and the caribou birthing grounds are crucial to their way of life. "We call this place where the caribou give birth Iizhik Gwat'an Gwandaii Goodlit," Sarah says, "which means 'The Sacred Place Where Life Begins.' "

Why is the Arctic coastal plain such a special birthplace? Abundant plant growth here in the spring nourishes pregnant and nursing caribou. Cooler temperatures along the Arctic Ocean delay the hatching of mosquitoes and biting flies, so the deer are undisturbed by the swarms of insects that will appear later. These unique conditions—and the fact that there are not many predators on the coastal plain—offer newborn caribou a good chance of surviving their vulnerable first few weeks of life.

In 1988, the Gwich'in people received some disturbing news: The coastal plain of the Arctic National Wildlife Refuge could soon be opened up to oil drilling. If that happened, new roads and pipelines would force the caribou that were pregnant or nursing to abandon their traditional birthing grounds—which could lead to the decline and eventual disappearance of the herd.

The people in the Gwich'in villages were gravely concerned about the threat to the Porcupine River caribou. They saw it as a threat to their own survival as well. "Our stories say that in ancient times, our people and the caribou shared the same heart," Sarah explains. "If you drill for oil here, you will be drilling into the heart of our people."

The Gwich'in elders called on the chiefs of all the villages—plus a delegation of the youth—to come together in an emergency meeting called a Gwich'in Niintsyaa, the first such gathering in more than a hundred years. The Gwich'in people decided to speak with one voice in opposition to oil and gas development in the birthing grounds of the Porcupine River caribou herd. Eight representatives were chosen to carry the message to the outside world. Sarah James was one of them.

With the support of the Gwich'in Nation and their friends, Sarah starting going out into the world to explain why drilling for oil on the coastal plain of the Arctic National Wildlife Refuge could harm the caribou herd and the way of life of her people. She travels the country, telling her story to environmental and human rights groups, students, and lawmakers. She brings journalists to Arctic Village to meet the Gwich'in people and better understand their way of life. She speaks at conferences around the world and has provided testimony to the U.S. Senate and House of Representatives.

Sarah James

"A birthplace needs to be quiet and clean," Sarah explains. "The oil companies say that they won't drill in the birthing season and that they'll pick up their gravel roads and leave everything the way it was. But no technology in the world can do this. They say they'll make ice roads instead of gravel roads, but there's no fresh water to do it with. They say that oil spills can be prevented. But there's no way that they can be prevented."

Alaska's Prudhoe Bay oil fields, just outside the Arctic National Wildlife Refuge

Sarah gives the example of Prudhoe Bay, the largest oil field in North America, located just outside the Arctic National Wildlife Refuge and only 60 miles (96 kilometers) west of the Porcupine River caribou birthing grounds. "There's an oil spill every day at Prudhoe Bay," she says. "Most of the spills are small, but the consequences are still big. The ground here is tundra, which is a delicate mix of grassland and water. Once oil seeps in, that part of the tundra will never recover."

The Arctic Refuge coastal plain is the most critical part of the delicate ecosystems that the Arctic National Wildlife Refuge was established to

Caribou in their birthing grounds by the Arctic Ocean
in the Arctic National Wildlife Refuge

protect. Many species besides the caribou give birth here—polar bears, grizzly bears, the Arctic fox, musk ox, and 150 kinds of birds. Birds nest here from every state in the United States and even from as far away as Antarctica.

Sarah also explains why drilling for oil in the refuge cannot solve the oil crisis. "There's less than a year's worth of U.S. oil consumption under the ground here—and it would take ten years to extract it."

She has educated large numbers of people, from ordinary citizens to elected officials, about the dangers of oil drilling in the wildlife refuge. Partly thanks to her work, the refuge is still protected. "They haven't drilled yet!" she says triumphantly.

Also, because of Sarah, the Gwich'in voice is being heard in the debate about oil drilling. Before Sarah began her work, hardly anybody knew about the Gwich'in people or thought they had anything to add to the debate about oil drilling. "Our rights to live off the land and provide for our families—the way our ancestors have done for thousands of years—are now part of the discussion."

Sarah's hope for the future is permanent protection from oil drilling in the Arctic National Wildlife Refuge. "People, animals, and plants all depend on a healthy environment to survive—together," she says. "When you look down, you can see that we are all standing on the same Earth."

TWELVE

Safeguarding the California Coast

"We are the future. The future is ours."
ERICA FERNANDEZ
Student and Environmental Activist
Oxnard, California

When 12-year-old Erica Fernandez volunteered to help clean up the beach in her new hometown, Oxnard, California, she could barely speak English. She had no idea then that within four years, her passionate speeches for the environment and social justice would inspire thousands of people to action—and help change the mind of the governor himself.

Back then, in 2003, she was just a kid helping 20 adults take care of the beach. She and her family had recently arrived in California from a small town in Mexico. "I always loved the ocean," she says, "so it made me really sad to see this beautiful beach full of trash. That's why I decided to help." Her dedication impressed the adults in the group. One woman—the only one who spoke Spanish—started explaining to Erica that something far more dangerous than trash threatened the beach.

There was a plan to build a processing station for liquefied natural gas 14 miles (22.5 kilometers) off the coast of Oxnard. It would be like a giant factory, 14 stories high and three football fields long, floating in the ocean. A pipeline 36 inches (almost a meter) in diameter—as big around as a hula hoop—would transport this highly explosive gas under the ocean to Oxnard, and then right through Erica's community.

"At first I couldn't believe it," she says. "I was really shocked. What if there was a leak or an explosion? People could get killed!" She asked around in her community and found out that nobody knew about the project. "We were going to be in danger from this facility, and the company wasn't even telling us about it." Erica started going to meetings with her friends from the beach cleanup to educate herself about what was happening.

Behind the new project was the largest mining company in the world, based in Australia. Their plan was to condense natural gas into a liquid by "supercooling" it to around −260° Fahrenheit

(−162° Centigrade), and then ship it to their new floating processing station off the Oxnard coast. There, the liquid would be heated up until it was a gas again and would be sent out via pipeline to customers in California and the Western Unites States.

The process would send over 200 tons (181 metric tons) of air pollution per year across the 14 miles (22.5 kilometers) of ocean to Erica's community. Not only that, the station would take in millions of gallons of seawater per day to cool its generators, and discharge the water more than 28 degrees Fahrenheit (15 degrees Centigrade) hotter than the surrounding ocean. This hot wastewater (called "thermal waste") would cause serious harm to the surrounding ecosystem, killing zooplankton (very tiny floating creatures) and small fish critical to the survival of marine mammals and fisheries.

"Their point of view was that it was a cheaper gas," Erica explains. "They never considered the health of the people. They never considered the safety issues. Their idea was just to make money, and that was all."

Erica started going door to door in her mainly Spanish-speaking farmworker community. She pointed out where the big gas pipeline

was going to cross people's yards and the fields where they worked. Escaping gas could cause an explosion and fire, she explained, and operations out in the ocean would make the air dirtier. People were already suffering because of pollution from a nearby power plant. "Many people had to use respirators to breathe, including my father. I didn't want to end up like that. I didn't think anybody should." Erica's neighbors were worried, but they didn't know what to do.

Erica didn't know either, but she cared too much to stay silent. Having grown up in the tiny town of Gómez Farías, in the Mexican state of Michoacán, she had a strong motivation to care for nature. "We grew our own food and raised our own animals. Taking care of nature was part of survival." She wanted to bring that same spirit to her new life in California.

She joined her friends in weekly protests at the office of the natural gas company. Prospects of stopping the project did not look good. The governor was in favor of it, and so were the powerful state commissions that would have to approve it. "The word on the street was that there was nothing we could do."

Behind the scenes, however, opposition was growing, and Erica was becoming the spokesperson for the youth of the town. As her English improved, she talked to kids in her high school about what was going on. She regularly walked her neighborhood along the route of the proposed pipeline, using a hula hoop to show people the size of the pipe that would pass by their houses and under their elementary school. She talked to church groups. She talked to the media, and stories about the dangers of the proposed facility began appearing in the press. She gathered a group of young supporters to come with her to demonstrations. Important environmental groups like the Sierra Club took notice and began helping with the campaign.

After four years of educating people about the dangers of the natural gas project, Erica was ready for the next step. The California Land Commission, which would rule on the natural gas company permit and review its environmental report, had scheduled a public meeting for April 9, 2007. In an amazing show of opposition to the project, Erica helped bring 3,000 people to a demonstration outside the commission offices. More than 300 of them were high school students.

Inside, Erica was one of the opposition speakers, representing the youth. "I didn't know if they would listen to me. My English wasn't good and I was only sixteen," she says. As she nervously approached the microphone, she was informed that time was running out. One minute and thirty seconds was all she had. "I couldn't give my prepared speech, so I just spoke from my heart."

NO FLOATING FACTORY!

LNG

LNG PROTECT OUR COAST!!

LNG

The result was electrifying. When Erica was finished, people stood up and broke into applause, even though clapping was not allowed at the hearings. One of the commissioners said, "I'm very moved by your testimony, Erica. When I was your age, I was playing video games." The commission voted 2–1 against the proposal.

Three days later, Erica spoke at a meeting of the California Coastal Commission, which oversees the well-being of the California coast. Again, her testimony was well received, as were the statements by other speakers from environmental and citizen groups. The commission voted 12–0 to reject the natural gas proposal.

Erica was jubilant, but she also knew that the governor's decision still lay ahead. Unless he also rejected the proposal, it would be approved. It was well known that he favored the project.

"We made thousands of phone calls and sent thousands of postcards telling the governor why this facility was a bad idea." In July 2007, the governor made an unexpected move: He vetoed the project. Erica and her friends had won! Other companies have since tried to push through similar projects, but now there are many more environmental requirements for approval—and Erica and the thousands of people she inspired are keeping watch.

Only the second person in her family to go to college, Erica wants to become an environmental lawyer so she can fight for the environment and for the rights of communities. She wants other young people to speak out when they see something wrong, even if they feel shy about it at first. She likes to quote the words of her role model, César Chávez: "We are the future. The future is ours."

Erica Fernandez

How You Can Get Involved

Kelydra Welcker and Erica Fernandez started their environmental work by doing beach cleanups.

John Todd spent hours watching how nature worked.

Alex Lin was looking for a project he could do with his classmates that would help his community.

If you're interested in being involved in an environmental effort, there are many ways you can get started. Like Kelydra Welcker and Erica Fernandez, you could work on a cleanup campaign in your neighborhood. Depending on where you live, this might mean picking up litter from a city park or beach, or it might mean helping to plant trees the way Barry Guillot and his students did.

It's amazing what you can learn about your environment when you pitch in to help improve it. Kelydra learned that a factory was releasing chemicals into the Ohio River. Erica found out about plans to build a natural gas processing plant that could hurt her community. You too might discover something that you are passionate about—a problem to solve or a new interest to explore.

Some people get involved with the environment by carefully watching how one process in nature works. John Todd did that. By looking at a stream flowing through different plants, he learned that nature has its own cleaning process. Later, he was able to use this knowledge to make his inventions. Is there something about the environment that you're really curious about? How can you learn more?

If you live in a community with a serious environmental problem—like a chemical plant or a landfill—then you might want to help bring attention to the situation so it can be addressed. The stories of Margie Richard and Erica Fernandez show how people can help resolve pollution problems by speaking up about them. Just as Erica did, you can begin by getting advice from adults and finding out what environmental groups are active in your community. Then see if you can help in their efforts.

Alex Lin and his classmates created a recycling program for electronic waste. Many communities have similar programs now. Find out where in your community you can take used computers and other electronic devices. What about disposing of smaller items like used batteries?

Will Allen's dream for the future is to grow food in many-story buildings. Julia Bonds wants to build windmills for energy so people will stop blowing up mountains for coal. Sarah James wants permanent protection for the Arctic National Wildlife Refuge in Alaska. What is your own environmental vision for the future? And how could you get started now?

ACKNOWLEDGMENTS

I want to thank all the heroes in this book who took the time to talk to me about their work and their hopes for the future. You are an inspiration!

And thank you to the many people and organizations who helped me find the heroes, sent me fabulous photographs, shared their expert knowledge, and advised and supported me at the very beginning of this project:

Sharon Smith, Program Director, New Leaders Initiative and Brower Youth Awards, Earth Island Institute; Barbara Ann Richman, Executive Director, The Barron Prize; Denny Larson, Executive Director, Global Community Monitor; Anne Rolfes, Founding Director, Louisiana Bucket Brigade; Katie Ferguson at Growing Power; Sonya Pichardo at Green Worker Cooperatives; Kim Sousa at Todd Ecological; Aida Navarro at WiLDCOAST; Barbara Poley, Executive Director, and Rowena Dickerson at The Hopi Foundation; Jacob Scherr from NRDC; Luci Beach, Executive Director, and Chris Cannon at the Gwich'in Steering Committee; Owen Bailey from the Sierra Club; Lupe Anguiano, Executive Director, Stewards of the Earth; Carmen Ramirez; and the members of the Coal River Mountain Watch network.

Thanks also to researchers Ricardo Niño and Laurel Potter; Lani Alo from the Goldman Environmental Prize; Vance Howard; Dr. Sumi Mehta; Rhea Suh; Hilda Castillo; Richard Rodriguez; Armando Nieto; librarian Sandy Schuckett; publishing gurus Susan McConnell, Peter Beren, and George Young; Wendy Lichtman; Maya Gonzalez; Mark Dukes; Cathleen O'Brien; Marina Drummer and the LEF Foundation; and Intersection for the Arts.

I'd also like to thank the following advisers: Dr. Raquel Rivera Pinderhughes, Oralia Garza de Cortés, Ana-Elba Pavon, Dr. Rosie Arenas, Dorothy Hearst, Azibuike Akaba, and Sandra Funke.

Finally, many thanks to Andrea Menotti, my dedicated editor at Chronicle Books, and to Doug Barasch from the Natural Resources Defense Council. And thank you to my husband and partner, David Schecter, who makes everything possible.

PHOTO CREDITS

Prudhoe Bay, Alaska

ARCTIC NATIONAL
WILDLIFE REFUGE

Arctic Village, Alaska

PORCUPINE RIVER

CANADA

UNITED
STATES

Oxnard, California

TIJUANA RIVER

Tijuana, Mexico

Hopi Indian
Reservation, Arizona

SAN IGNACIO LAGOON

SEA OF CORTEZ

MEXICO

Mexico City, Mexico

Milwaukee,
Wisconsin

Chicago,
Illinois

OHIO RIVER

Woods Hole, Massachusetts
Westerly, Rhode Island
New York City, New York

APPALACHIAN MOUNTAINS

Parkersburg, West Virginia
Whitesville, West Virginia

Old Diamond, Louisiana
Destrehan, Louisiana

MISSISSIPPI RIVER

LOUISIANA
WETLANDS

GULF OF MEXICO